VIOLIN

HAL•LEONARD
INSTRUMENTAL
PLAY-ALONG

Disney

Hannah Montana

How To Use The CD Accompanimen[...]
The CD is playable on any CD play[...]
MAC users, the CD is enhanced sc[...]
the recording to any tempo withou[...]

A melody cue appears on the right channel only. If [...]
CD player has a balance adjustment, you can adjust the
volume of the melody by turning down the right channel.

ISBN 978-1-4234-6106-7

Walt Disney Music Company
Wonderland Music Company, Inc.

DISTRIBUTED BY

HAL•LEONARD®
CORPORATION

7777 W. BLUEMOUND RD. P.O. BOX 13819 MILWAUKEE, WI 53213

In Australia Contact:
Hal Leonard Australia Pty. Ltd.
4 Lentara Court
Cheltenham, Victoria, 3192 Australia
Email: ausadmin@halleonard.com.au

Visit Hal Leonard Online at
www.halleonard.com

◆ BEST OF BOTH WORLDS

VIOLIN

Words and Music by MATTHEW GERRARD
and ROBBIE NEVIL

BIGGER THAN US

VIOLIN

Words and Music by TIM JAMES
and ANTONINA ARMATO

D.S. al Coda

CODA

❸ FIND YOURSELF IN YOU

Words and Music by MATTHEW GERRARD,
AMBER HEZLEP, JULIA ROSS
and SARAH ROSS

VIOLIN

◆ I GOT NERVE

VIOLIN

Words and Music by JEANNIE LURIE,
KEN HAUPTMAN and ARUNA ABRAMS

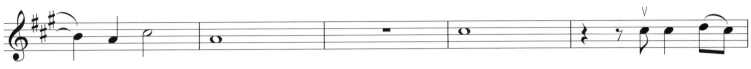

⬥5 I LEARNED FROM YOU

Words and Music by MATTHEW GERRARD
and STEVE DIAMOND

VIOLIN

13

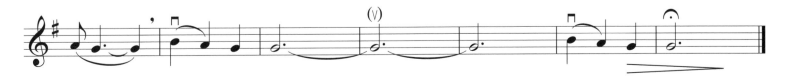

◆ JUST LIKE YOU

VIOLIN

Words and Music by ANDREW DODD
and ADAM WATTS

◆7 LIFE'S WHAT YOU MAKE IT

Words and Music by MATTHEW GERRARD
and ROBBIE NEVIL

VIOLIN

Lively Pop

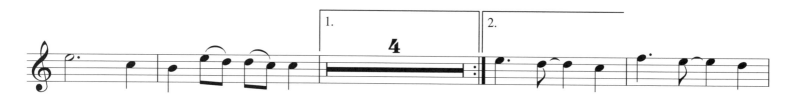

◆8 NOBODY'S PERFECT

VIOLIN

Words and Music by MATTHEW GERRARD
and ROBBIE NEVIL

♦9 OLD BLUE JEANS

VIOLIN

Words and Music by MICHAEL BRADFORD
and PAM SHEYNE

◆⑩ PUMPIN' UP THE PARTY

Words and Music by
JAMIE HOUSTON

VIOLIN

◆11 ONE IN A MILLION

VIOLIN

Words and Music by TOBY GAD
and NEGIN DJAFARI

♦12 THE OTHER SIDE OF ME

Violin

Words and Music by MATTHEW GERRARD,
ROBBIE NEVIL and JAY LANDERS

Funky Pop

◆13 ROCK STAR

VIOLIN

Words and Music by JEANNIE LURIE,
ARIS ARCHONTIS and CHEN NEEMAN

WE GOT THE PARTY

Words and Music by
KARA DioGUARDI

VIOLIN

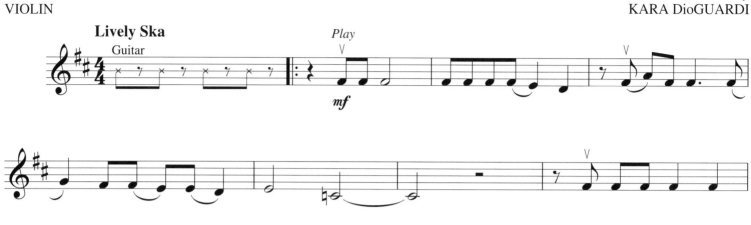

TRUE FRIEND

VIOLIN

Words and Music by
JEANNIE LURIE